I Can Make a Difference

Helping the Environment

Vic Parker

Heinemann Library
Chicago, Illinois

www.capstonepub.com
Visit our website to find out more information about Heinemann-Raintree books.

To order:
☎ Phone 888-454-2279
🖥 Visit www.capstonepub.com
  to browse our catalog and order online.

Edited by Daniel Nunn, Rebecca Rissman, and Sian Smith
Designed by Steve Mead
Picture research by Ruth Blair
Production by Eirian Griffiths
Originated by Capstone Global Library Ltd
Printed and bound in the United States of America, North Mankato, MN

15 14 13 12
10 9 8 7 6 5 4 3 2

Library of Congress Cataloging-in-Publication Data
Parker, Victoria.
  Helping the environment / Victoria Parker.
    p. cm.—(I can make a difference)
  Includes bibliographical references and index.
ISBN 978-1-4329-5946-3 (hb)
ISBN 978-1-4329-5951-7 (pb)
1. Environmentalism—Juvenile literature. 2. Voluntarism—Juvenile literature. I. Title.
  GE195.5.P37 2010
  363.7—dc22   2011015689

042012
006629RP

Acknowledgments
We would like to thank the following for permission to reproduce photographs: Corbis pp. 6 (© Juice Images), 15 (© Karin Dreyer/Blend Images), 16 (© Charles Gullung), 19 (© amanaimages), 22 (© JGI/Jamie Grill/Blend Images), 23 (© Aliki Salmas/First Light), 25 (Mike Kemp/In Pictures); Getty Images p. 10 (Max Oppenheim); iStockphoto pp. 7 (© Rich Legg), 17 (© cstar55), 26 (© luoman); Photolibrary pp. 11, 21 (Peter Arnold Images), 29 (Peter Bennett/Ambient Images); Shutterstock pp. 4, 14, 27 (© Monkey Business Images), 8 (© Picsfive), 9 (© Morgan Lane Photography), 12 (© Adisa), 13 (© Geoffrey Kuchera), 18 (© Michael William), 20 (© Brenda Carson), 24 (© Velychko).

Cover photograph of children picking up litter on a beach reproduced with permission of Getty Images (Fuse).

Every effort has been made to contact copyright holders of any material reproduced in this book. Any omissions will be rectified in subsequent printings if notice is given to the publisher.

Contents

Some words are shown in bold, **like this**. You can find out what they mean by looking in the glossary.

Why Help?

Volunteering means spending your time and energy being helpful. Many places, people, and animals need all sorts of help. By helping, we can make the world a better, happier place.

Anyone can volunteer to help, young or old.

Knowing that you have been helpful can make you feel really good.

Volunteering can also give you the chance to:

- go to new places

- meet new people

- learn new skills

- get some exercise

- have fun!

  Before you help anyone, always get permission from a parent or guardian.

How Can I Help the Environment?

The **environment** can be your local area. The environment can also be Planet Earth, and all the animals, plants, and materials in our world.

Your local environment might be a city, a town, or the countryside.

Many things harm our planet, but there are lots of ways we can help the environment. For example, cars produce fumes that make the air dirty. You can **reduce** the number of cars on the road by sharing lifts, or traveling by bus or train, whenever you can.

Walking and cycling are even better for the environment, because they produce no **pollution** at all.

Reduce, Reuse, Recycle

We all make lots of garbage, and getting rid of this can harm the **environment**. Garbage that is buried can leak poisons into the earth. Garbage that is burned can release poisons into the air.

The garbage each person in the US makes in a year can weigh the same as the largest polar bears!

You could make it your job to collect and sort your family's recycling.

You can help make less garbage by **volunteering** to **reduce**, **reuse**, and **recycle**. Reducing means using fewer things. Reusing means using things again if you can. Recycling means turning used things into new things.

Compost Corner

You can **volunteer** to collect some types of your family's leftover food to use for compost, such as vegetable peelings, salad, fruit scraps, and egg shells. But don't collect meat, fish, dairy products, rice, pasta, citrus fruit, or beans.

Only collect the right types of unwanted food, or your volunteering will be unhelpful.

Put this waste into a special container, or composter. The waste will rot into a mulch called compost, which is great used in yards to help plants grow well.

You can put waste, from yard work, such as grass cuttings and leaves, into a composter, too.

Looking Out for Litter

Litter in our **environment** can harm humans, other animals, or plants. For example, a plastic bag dumped in a stream could trap a duck. A glass bottle dropped in a park could cut a child playing football.

As well as being harmful, litter also looks terrible.

Always wear gloves and protective clothing when you are picking up litter.

You can help improve your environment by **volunteering** to pick up litter. There might be a local "clean-up" day you could join in with, or you could get some grown-ups and friends together and hold your own.

 Never pick up broken glass – tell an adult if you find some.

Grow Your Own

Much of our food comes from far away, such as peas from Africa and bananas from the Caribbean. The airplanes and trucks that bring us our food use up Earth's precious **fuels** and these are running out fast.

Food choices can harm or help the **environment**.

Help by choosing to buy food that has been grown close to home.

Volunteering to grow fruit and vegetables will help to save our planet's **raw materials**. Ask if you can use a corner of your yard, or have plant pots on your windowsill.

Plant a Tree

Trees are very important for our planet because their leaves clean the air that we breathe. Their roots help to clean the soil, too. The more trees there are on Earth, the better.

Trees are extremely useful, as well as beautiful.

You could **volunteer** to plant a new tree in your local area. Ask a grown-up to help you find a tree-planting project you can take part in. Ask your family, a friend, or your school if you can help them plant a tree.

Planting a tree can be very rewarding.

Don't Waste Water

There is not enough clean water for everyone and everything living on Earth, so it is important to save it when you can. You could help by turning the faucet off while you brush your teeth.

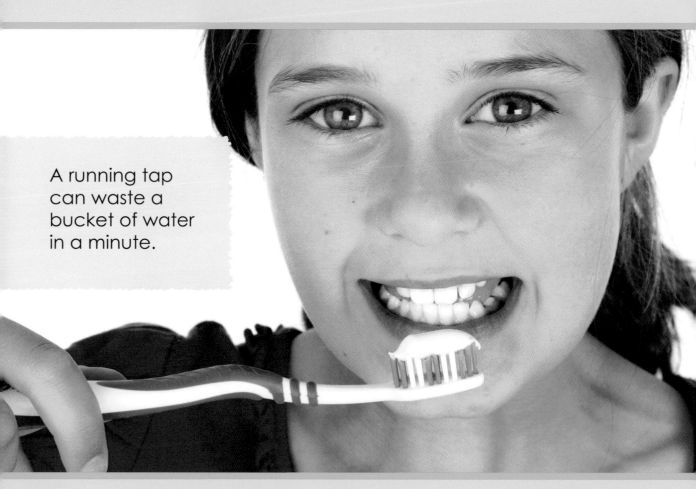

A running tap can waste a bucket of water in a minute.

If you have a normal shower, you could also help by having a shower instead of a bath. A shower uses much less water. But be careful, as having a very long shower can use more water than having a bath.

A short shower uses much less water than a bath.

Donating

Do you have any toys, games, or clothes you no longer need? You could give these to thrift stores that use the money they get to help **environmental charities**. Giving up your things in this way is called **donating**.

Make sure the things you donate are still in good condition.

When it is your birthday, you could ask your family and friends to donate money to your favorite **environmental** or **conservation** group instead of buying you a present. You could ask for membership to the group as your gift.

Many groups that work to help the environment need money to keep going.

Thinking Small

Often, small things can help the **environment** in big ways. For instance, you could **volunteer** to go around your house regularly turning off lights that aren't in use. This saves Earth's **fuels**, that are used to make electricity.

You can turn off lights, computers, and televisions that aren't being used.

Sometimes, it is helpful to volunteer *not* to do things, too. For instance, if you are cold at home, you could decide *not* to use extra energy by turning the heating up. You could put a thick sweater on instead.

You could also save energy by choosing *not* to watch television. Try reading, drawing, or playing a game instead.

Thinking Big

You might feel strongly about a particular local **environmental** issue, such as tidying and replanting an overgrown vacant lot in your local area. If so, you will need to ask lots of people to help you.

Doing things on your own can be fun, but it is hard work!

If you get together in a group, you can raise money to help your local environmental cause, too. For example, you could do a **sponsored** event. This is where people promise to give you money for completing a challenge, like walking around a park several times.

Holding a yard sale is a great way to raise money.

Thinking Even Bigger

You might also feel strongly about an **environmental** issue that affects the whole planet. For example, you might want to try to stop people cutting down trees in the Amazon rain forest in South America.

Millions of trees are being cut down in rain forests every year.

You could write a letter about an environmental issue to the **politicians** who are in charge of countries.

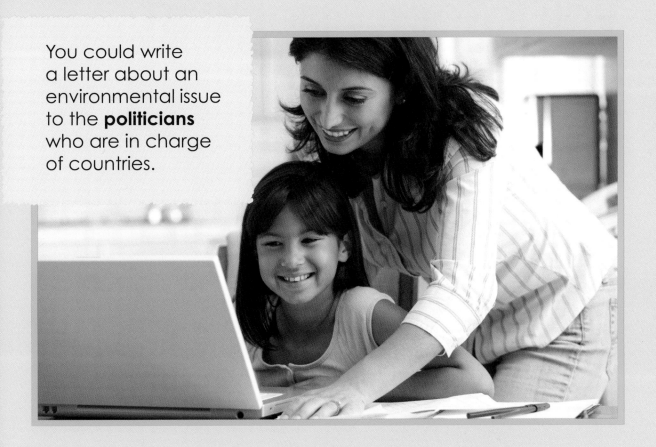

You can **volunteer** support by telling others about these issues and asking them to help too. Try making badges or posters, or even putting on a short play about the problem for your family and friends.

Volunteer Checklist

To be a good **volunteer**, you need to:

- think of others

- listen well and suggest ideas

- be interested and have lots of energy

- share and take turns, if you are in a team

- keep your promises

- be friendly.

Most importantly, *always* check with your parent or guardian before you volunteer to help outside your home. Then they can make sure that you will be safe. They may even want to help!

Working with other people you know well can be a safe way to volunteer.

Glossary

charity an organization that helps others

conservation protecting animals and the environment from harm

donate to give away something that is of use to someone else

environment world around us

environmental to do with the environment

fuels materials such as oil, coal, gas, and wood which can be used to make energy

politicians people who are in charge of running countries

pollution when the soil, air, or water is damaged by a harmful substance

raw materials materials found in nature which other things can be made from

recycle break down materials and use them again to make new things

reduce cut down on the amount of something

reuse use something again

sponsor to pay money to help with something, such as the care of an animal

volunteer offer to do something. Someone who offers to do something is called a volunteer.

Find Out More

Books

Ganeri, Anita. *Something Old, Something New: Recycling (You Can Save the Planet)*. Chicago: Raintree, 2006.

Olien, Rebecca. *75 Ways to Make a Difference for People, Animals, and the Environment (Kids Care!)*. Danbury, Conn.: Ideals Publishing Corporation, 2007.

O'Sullivan, Joanne. *101 Ways You Can Help Save the Planet Before You're 12!* Ashville, N.C.: Lark Books, 2009.

Websites

kidshealth.org/kid/feeling/thought/volunteering.html
Find out about how families can volunteer.

pbskids.org/itsmylife/emotions/volunteering
This website will help you think about how you could begin volunteering.

www.volunteermatch.org/
This website has details of thousands of organizations which need volunteers.

Index